Minimalist Budget

*Complete Guide on
How to Manage your Money.*

*Best Strategies on
How To Save Money,
Spend Less and Stay Debt-Free*

Jeffrey Turpen

DEDICATION

We dedicate this book to our family,
our parents and children.

Table of Content

Introduction

In the modern world of money is the basis of our society. Thanks to the money a person can live his life, develop all his projects and create a family. Money is indispensable for living our dreams and fulfilling our primary needs (i.e., food, housing, and clothing) and the secondary ones (or our whims, passions, and pastimes, such as travel or electronic gadgets). Without the money, you cannot meet any of these needs.

But the money always seems never to be enough. The monthly fixed expenses are so many (food, bills, transport) and the unexpected (e.g., car breakdown or PC, a visit to the dentist) are always around the corner. How can we manage our money well enough to save enough to enjoy the so-called financial freedom and not arrive at the end of the month at the limit of bankruptcy?

Solutions to save money are different, and also systems to earn money fast.

If you want to risk ending up in prison, you can start to deal drugs, sell weapons or other illegal activities. They are activities that bring a lot of money if you can create a small empire. You may also hire employees and stay home while your minions peddle your drugs and live a life of luxury.

All these until you get arrested or killed by some rival.

Or you could try to become a stock market operator, trying to imitate Leonardo Di Caprio in "The Wolf Of Wall Street" and create a millionaire empire. Working on the stock market seems easy, online tutorials explain how to earn huge numbers in no time, failure is impossible.

Then you will only find bad investments, and you will lose all your money.

You can also try to enter the online betting market. You are a soccer or football enthusiast, you know all the background, and you always know the result of all the matches. You could monetize this passion, bet so much money on an absurd result, sooner or later you will win a bet, and you will earn a lot of money, it's easy to study a reliable system, and you will always win.

But in the end, you will always lose all your bets. The victories will be extremely rare, and eventually, you'll lose a lot more money than you earn.

These three examples are ironic, but the message is unequivocal: there is no way to make money easy, or at least not in a legal way. Money must always be earned through a job. In this book, we will also explore systems to round off your revenue with extra activities, but the primary focus of your economy must be the proper management of your current finances.

Managing your finances in the best way is the first step to achieving financial freedom. Manage your money in the best way, and you will have the impression that you have double your money.

What is financial freedom?

To put it simply, it is the economic availability you have to be able to live your lifestyle without worrying about money. To obtain a real financial freedom, your money saves every month must exceed at least 50% the total amount of your expenses. This way you can deal with in the best way all the unexpected costs and satisfy your whims.

The best way to achieve financial freedom is to diversify your income (i.e., having different sources of revenue) and to manage in the best way the expenses and all your monthly budget.

Diversifying investments is very important because it will allow you to have different gains that can amortize a loss of income or an unexpected event.

How can you achieve this financial freedom?

In addition to learning to manage your monthly budget, you will need to diversify your investments. An excellent way to expand investment and to have different sources of revenue is to take advantage of the Internet and all the opportunities it offers.

Start an online business by selling items on Ebay or Amazon, or use of Amazon's affiliate program through your Facebook profile or your blog. Identify a niche that you like (your passion is perfect) and started to talk about this sector, by publicizing the more popular products at that time. The affiliate program consists of a link that will direct users to the advertised product, and the program will recognize you a percentage of the sale.

Or you can start a career as a freelancer on popular sites such as Guru or Up work if you are a good translator, graphic designer or SEO talented.

If you enjoy writing, you can publish an ebook on Kindle and earn money on every sale, or you can create a YouTube channel and earn through advertising inserted in your video. The possibilities the Internet offers to have an extra income are many and very valid. But these activities need time to start to be a valuable source of revenue, and you will need to have a large audience and many visitors, many like and contacts that will allow you to have enough advertising revenue.

Chapter 1- Why Is It Important to Budget?

Establish a monthly budget for expenses is essential for every business and every person. The budget allows us to have an idea of the money that we can spend every day and in this way it is possible to assess whether a spending is needed or whether it is superfluous.

Many people, however, do not like to establish a budget because they believe that this activity is limiting and somewhat humiliating for them. This attitude is wrong and harmful because it is just a way to avoid facing this problem. Also, many people are suffering from "compelling shopping" (we'll talk about it in detail later) and having a limited budget is their worst nightmare.

How can you set a proper budget for each month?

Firstly, it is necessary to carefully monitor the costs incurred during the previous months and try to find an average figure. Bills and expenses for food. An average is a good start to try to figure out the initial value of our budget, that is, the figure we will spend each month, our fixed fee.

To this number it is necessary to add the expenses for the superfluous and the unforeseen, so the original figure must be increased considerably. Analyze your extra expenses and start to wonder if they are essential and which ones you want to save. Delete the activities you feel unnecessary before setting up your monthly budget and thus have already eliminated a large source of waste.

The monthly budget does not have to be strictly necessary to pay for your expenses, but it must also allow you to face extra fees or a whim, even just to motivate you to meet this limit. Afford an impulse, an ice cream or an extra pizza is the prize to fit your monthly budget and must be fair to be rewarded

Do not interpret this monthly budget as a strict limit, but as a guideline for your expenses. If you can not respect this budget for some reasons, do not worry, analyzed the problems that forced you to overcome your budget and assessed the possibility to increase it if these issues were to become constant. If, however, you can keep up with the budget you will have to understand whether you have been able to do so easily or with sacrifices. In the first case, keep your budget, otherwise increase it.

If you can meet the budget, give yourself a prize, for example, a day at the wellness center, or a cake or a crazy spending, if it is not excessive. This award will encourage you to respect your budget and work as a psychological motivator, a reward for doing a good job.

Chapter 2 - Traps of Minimalism

If you look closely at your home, you will certainly find many items that can be classified as unnecessary.

What is the utility of all the ornaments you have?

Having ten pairs of shoes is required?

Do not you think all the food you have in the fridge is excessive?

Can you live without an expensive smartphone?

These are the first questions that came to my mind, and if you want to start saving and respecting your budget, you will have to begin your spending review from your home.

So first you start listing all the useless items you have at home and think about when you bought them and if you are still buying them.

This is a great starting point. We often buy items just for the pleasure of buying them or because we like them at that time, but when we get home, they prove to be useless.

The second step is to analyze the expenses that you support out of the house, the coffee in the morning, the candy, a drink with friends, cigarettes. They are small charges, but in a month, they can become substantial and make you spend a lot of money.

Here too you should begin to wonder if these expenses are needed.

An aperitif per week instead of every day? Start to quit smoking? Less sweet?

Often these habits are not good for our health, because often when we are out of the house, we eat a lot of junk food that is harmful to our health.

In practice, you have to analyze all your expenses and start a real war against all the waste. This does not mean never indulging in a cake or spending, but not spending money every day for things that in the end do not serve us.

This cost control operation is defined by someone "Minimalism."

But what is the "Minimalism"?

We can define minimalism as a lifestyle where we try to avoid the waste and all the useless things. The necessary minimum is more than enough to be able to live a normal life.

The advantage of this way of life (at least in its intentions) is to focus only on necessities and save in this way time, money and energy.

For example, do not buy every year a new mobile phone model because "we do not need" is minimalist, not decorate your home with unnecessary items and do not observe the mode is minimalist.

Living with the indispensable minimum, only with the strictness necessary to live the lifestyle we want.

Presented in this way, the Minimalist lifestyle is desirable and above all allows you to save a lot of money.

But many people are enemies of this lifestyle that in the end does not allow to enjoy the joys of life thoroughly and to flaunt. Flaunt is the exact opposite of minimalism and consist of showing to everyone, in an obvious and exaggerated manner your wealth and the things that you own. Imagine for a moment being in a trendy place and looking at people. Branded dresses, watches, expensive smartphones, jewelry, sports cars.

All this can be translated into a scream "Hey, I have the money, look at me."

The people who flaunt believe that minimalism is a lifestyle worthy of a homeless, life is short, and yu have all the right to flaunt your money and your power.

The Minimalists, on the other hand, believe that flaunting is just a way to satisfy the ego and to humiliate other people, or "I am rich, you are poor, you are inferior."

Obviously, as in all aspects of life, there is no "just" lifestyle and a "wrong" way of life. Everyone has the right to live his life as best he believes until he harms other people.

The minimalism is a trap, to confine with stinginess.

We all know that "the stingy" is a comic caricature in many works (e.g., Uncle Scrooge in Disney) and in society is viewed with a mix of pity and sorrow. Being minimalist is very close to being considered a greedy person, and you have to avoid this error.

How can you avoid it?

Thanks to proper budget management. The budget must allow you to live well, to be able to deal with the unexpected expense but at the same time should not be wasted with stupid purchases.

If you succeed in establishing the right budget, you can be minimalist and avoid being stingy, because you will have the money to do what you want.

You will understand that you have reached a budget that suits the minimalist lifestyle when you can save all the months. Many sportsmen in their autobiographies have said the same thing "it is not important how much you earn, but only how much you can save."

Saving all the months on the budget is the best proof that you've managed to adopt the minimalist style without becoming Uncle Scrooge.

Similarly, minimalism can be adopted throughout your lifestyle.

How many friends are really "real"? How many can only be defined as "knowledge"?

How many activities in your day are just a waste of time?

By applying minimalism, you can select the friendships that interest you, the ones that are genuine and last for a long time, avoiding wasting time with people who do not want your company in any way. Real friendships during life are really few, and you'll be surprised to find that time is capable of erasing friendships that you believed stable.

It is better to have few friendships, but sincere and honest, "less is more."

Also, analyze the activities you do during the day. Many are a waste of time. How much time do you spend on Facebook? How much time do you lose every day in front of the smartphone?

You could use that time to study, for sport or personal growth activities.

Delete any loss of time is significant to be minimal because the time is saved during the day can be used in a much more productive way.

This does not mean you cannot afford a leisure time during the day, distracting and relieve stress is significant, but this activity does not take too long. Otherwise, it becomes procrastination, a great enemy of the minimalist lifestyle.

Chapter 3 - The Psychology Of Purchasing

Buying something is not an activity that is limited to the exchange of money in the store, but it is an activity that has great psychological implications. There are scientific studies used by large companies to sell their products. Very often these are psychological manipulations that push us to choose their product instead of the product of their competitors.

This activity does not only consist of creating a successful advertising campaign but in well-defined psychological techniques.

To be able to meet your budget, you will have to learn to know your "enemy" and know how to recognize these manipulation techniques when you see them.

First, look at the layout of the products in the supermarket. All the advertised products are placed in the front row, eye-catching to be immediately recognized and to encourage the purchase. Products that are cheaper or are not advertised at that time are placed up or down on the shelf, so they will not be displayed immediately and therefore try to sell them less.

The music in supermarkets has a vital function, that of putting us in a good mood (the songs are always commercial and danceable) and to encourage us to do so in the purchase. In the supermarket you will never find rock songs or melancholy tracks, but only the latest commercial hits and the most transmitted radio songs.

After all, a sad melody does not bother in any way to buy a bundle of biscuits, right?

Another great method to encourage the purchase is the price. Often, the price at which a product is sold is artificially inflated and then discounted at its true price, thus creating a "discount" that encourages the purchase. But actually, it's all a staging to look cheaper than the competitor.

An example to better understand this concept (an episode I witnessed).

A computer system vendor has an interview with a customer to sell his product and uses this psychological trick.

The product costs $ 100. This seller offers the customer the $ 200 product, and the customer says he is interested, but the price is too high. The seller then pretends to try to make a special discount "only for you" and propose the product to $ 100. A discount of 50%, the real deal, impossible not to accept these favorable conditions.

The customer buys the product believing that he is privileged and has made the best deal in his career, but in fact, he has been cheated or at least fooled, making him believe in a discount that does not exist.

This trick has many risks (sooner or later someone will notice the scam) but if the seller or the store has a big round of customers will be able to sell a lot before being discovered.

Think of the period of sales in the shops; there are a lot of scams because shopkeepers show unmatched discounts (60/70%) and leave the price unchanged.

By using the Internet and specific sites that compare prices you can try to avoid these scams.

Another price trick is to propose different price packages (with different features) to make the product more attractive, especially the product "in the middle."

A quick example.

A conference with several package deals.

The first package costs $ 100 and includes a photo with the guest, an autograph, the front row seat and a brunch. It seems very convenient.

The second package costs $ 300 and includes the same options as the first package, with the addition of a 10 minutes exclusive interview with the guest and a photo with a personalized dedication. $ 300 is a lot of money; most people will not buy this package because the price difference is high and does not offer much more than the first package.

But there is a quick way to make this package much more appealing and attractive, insert a third package at a higher price.

This is the third package, $ 500, which includes all the services already offered by the addition of a personal video call with the guest and an autographed shirt. Thanks to this trick, the $ 300 package becomes very competitive and will be purchased by more people. If you add another package, for example, $ 750, then the $ 500 package will become competitive.

This psychological trick is very useful because it makes a product that costs $ 300 attractive. If we stop for a moment thinking we would realize that $ 300 is a lot of money, and the $ 100 package is the cheapest one, but the psychological trick leads us to believe that the real deal is the $ 300 package.

Even Steve Jobs used a similar method to announce the birth of the first iPad model.

The Apple founder announced the technical features of the innovative product to the world while "$ 999" was written on a big screen.

The audience did not seem too interested, the product was excellent and innovative, but the price was too high. But Jobs, with a twist, announced that "$999" was the commercial value of the product, but not the selling price.

At that moment the price on the screen changed and became "$ 499", and the whole room exploded in great joy. A perfect psychological manipulation, an example of the first trick I've described.

$ 499 is a lot of money, but Steve Jobs has turned this figure into a big deal thanks to his powerful ability.

These are just some of the tricks that are being studied every day to try to sell a product. We must be aware of these techniques (they are not illegal, but they can be annoying) not to be cheated and buy everything we want without destroying our monthly budget.

Chapter 4 - How to Ignore Advertisements

Advertising is the soul of commerce and oxygen for every business.

Henry Ford said that every penny invested in advertising was a significant investment, and he was right.

Without advertising is impossible to get noticed on the market and you can't buy a product if you don't know that it exists. All the major companies in the world spend millions of dollars every month for advertising, hiring Hollywood directors, actors and the most paid sports stars for advertising their products.They made viral campaigns on the Internet and posters in all large cities to promote a product. With the right advertising campaign, every product has high chances of being sold.

But advertising can become very invasive and annoying.

How to ignore advertising?

It seems like an impossible mission, but with some tricks, we can ignore it.

On the Internet, we can use specialized software such as AdBlock Plus. This program is an add-on to the most modern browsers, such as Mozilla Firefox or Google Chrome and blocks all pop-up ads that appear while surfing the web. It also hides most of the banner ads that appear on websites.

Many people hate these programs because they hide the advertising of their sites, preventing them from gaining money, but at the same time, all users use them because banners and pop-ups are very annoying and often hide unwanted malware and viruses.

To install it just download it from the Web Store or through a Google search, it's free and does not slow down your browsing or computer work in any way.

About television advertising for me, there are only two solutions; the first is to subscribe to a pay TV, where the advertisements are reduced or change channels during commercials.

These solutions are two remedies that do not have much effect but are the only ones that can be applied.

For telephone advertising (phone calls to promote the products) you can enter the numbers that call you on the ignore list of your smartphone and prevent the usual number to bother you with persistent and annoying calls. If these numbers were to insist on calling, you could contact the police or a lawyer specializing in consumer rights to be compensated and to sue the companies.

But the real effective remedy for advertising is to have the right mental approach, to be aware of the things we need and that everything else is superfluous.

Think of your monthly budget and how much you can spend, and you will avoid buying many advertised products. You can do it sometimes but not always because otherwise you would fall into the trap of the advertisers and their manipulation will be successful.

You do not have to think that advertising is a bad thing, it is essential for commerce, many businesses can earn money and sell their products or services through advertising. Advertisers are just doing their job designing slogans, skits, and songs that remain in the head and that encourage people to buy their product.

In the end, it's just business, and if you think it's a war, well, you're wrong. You need to be aware of what you want and don't be influenced by the ads you see. You will only have to buy a product if you wish, not because you have been affected by advertising.

Chapter 5 - How to Get Over Compulsive Spending Habits

Shopping is not a bad thing, it's fair to buy the things we want, and we need, it is also a valuable psychological incentive to work and buy an item after so much work and so much sacrifice is a great satisfaction for us, is a prize to our work and our commitment.

But like everything we have to be careful not to overdo it. Compulsive shopping is a problem that can have massive repercussions on your budget and your family.

What is compulsive shopping?

In a few words, it is the uncontrollable and irrepressible impulse that leads us to buy a series of objects that we do not need, that we do not use or don't interest us. But at that moment we can not help but buy them.

Why?

This is a psychological disorder where the person gets satisfaction from buying objects. The pleasure is momentary and relives it must buy something new. Also, the person feels rich and powerful, without any problems.

In the most severe cases, this disorder can lead to kleptomania, or to steal objects just for the emotion this theft manages to generate within us.

This problem to be solved needs a course of treatment recommended by a doctor, drugs for mood control and group therapy.

But I can suggest a couple of remedies that can limit a compulsive purchase.

The first method is to never bring cash with us, or just the minimum necessary for purchases. The monthly budget is likely to be affected by this habit and has only a little money available is an effective deterrent to purchases.

However, a compulsive person can use a credit card to buy something, especially online, and this brings us to the second method, i.e., depriving the person of his credit card, to be replaced with a prepaid card to be charged each time after purchase. In this way, the person will have to waste time to recharge the prepaid card and take the money out of the monthly budget. Thanks to this stratagem only the most necessary purchases will go to closing.

I have tried this system first, and I can witness its effectiveness. In this way I was able to significantly limit my shopping online, saving a lot of money.

My remedy is simple and almost amateurish, the first thing to do when you are dealing with this problem is to recognize that you have a problem and seek help from a professional. This issue is very similar to gambling addiction and can lead to negative consequences for the whole family and budget.

Admit that you have this issue and asking for help is the first step to solving it (this is real in all areas of life) while ignoring the problem will only result to increase it and lead to far worse consequences.

Your budget and all the sacrifices made to respect it might be invalid because of this problem. This is a real war, do you want to win it or just waste time and continue buying unnecessary items every day?

The battle will be difficult, but you have to win at all costs.

Chapter 6 - Budgeting Methods

Now things get interesting.

In this chapter, we will discuss how you can keep up with the monthly budget and be able to save at the same time.

It is not difficult and does not require spells or absurd solutions, but only attention, intelligence, and strategy.

Step # 1: Plan

We have already said that we need to study the figure that suits our budget carefully. This study should not be superficial but will take time. Do not take this step lightly, because it is the basis to save money.

A careful planning of your budget will allow you to respect it without making any sacrifices while underestimating this and relying on intuition or overflow calculus will turn into a boomerang, and you will soon find yourself budgeting.

Prepare a paper table or Excel file and record all your monthly earnings, try to establish a history of at least one year. If you are employed, it will be very easy, because the salary will be roughly the same. The factor that will make a difference will be the extra work you will do (if you want to do them).

If you are self-employed, it is more difficult because the money you earn every month will not be constant but will depend on many variables. Try to find a medium in this case to establish an adequate budget.

Once you have set your monthly income, you will have to adjust the budget.

Take another excel file and try to record all of your monthly expenses, dividing them into three categories: Fixed, Flexible, optional.

The fixed costs are the same every month and may be the home loan, the rent, the car payments, spending on car insurance or medical insurance, the bills and the subscription to a service, such as a gym or the Metro.

These charges will be featured every month and represent an unavoidable expense to consider in your budget.

Flexible expenses are expenses that are constant, but you can decide how much money to spend. These are the costs for food, household, services that we buy during the month. These are expenses we can handle; we can decide whether to purchase a biscuit package instead of two, how much soap to buy and so on.

Optional expenses are those that are not necessary for survival. It's the money we spend on pastimes such as cinema, for our whims and all the superfluous.

If these expenses are starting to be too many are the first that need to be resized.

Once you determine, the amount of the three fees, deduct it from your monthly income.

That is the maximum budget. Resize it according to needs (by sacrificing optional expenses and reducing the flexible ones) and here is the monthly budget to use.

Step # 2: Spend smartly

Now you have established your budget. Now you have to respect it. It is not difficult if you use your brain and put some small tricks in practice.

First, decide where to cut the costs (flexible and optional expenses). You do not need to buy clothes every month, you do not need to buy sweets every week, and you do not need to go out every night to get drunk.

Many of these habits are also harmful to your health, and therefore this cost cut is also great for your body.

Prepare a shopping list every time you go to the supermarket and try to respect it without making any additional purchases. Obviously, may happen that the list is not perfect and during the shopping, you will notice products that are not on the list, but you need it. You can buy them, but this exception should never become the rule. Extra charges outside the list are deadly enemies of our budget.

Buy the products that are in stock and have great discounts in this way you will save money purchasing whatever you need.

Do not buy the products of the major brands, but those of the supermarket or the equivalent products of smaller brands. The product is the same, but quality too and you will also save up to 10%.

Buy fresh products (especially meat) and if you are afraid not to consume them, put the meat in the freezer before the expiration date. Schedule the week's menu to avoid buying too many fresh products such as meat to avoid risking them getting outdated.

Buy larger quantities of the products you use. If you find the King Size package of your favorite cookies, buy it rather than the regular package, or a bottle of oil or a maxi-pack of Yogurt. But you must be sure to consume the product before the expiration date otherwise this purchase will be useless.

Abandon your vices.

Stop smoking (think about how much money you will save and your health!).

Do not gamble

Do not get drunk

Never fall into the traps of advertising.

Buy a bulk of online products; you will often find exceptional wholesale offers.

This is a testimony of this system, which took place yesterday.

A friend was about to buy condoms for sex with his girlfriend, and I accompanied her to the vending machine. The product cost $ 8, and the box contained six condoms.

The cost was not cheap.

I said, "Why do not you buy wholesale on Amazon instead of buying this product?"

He did a search through the Amazon App and found the same product on offer. 50 Condoms for $ 22, Free Shipping with Amazon Prime. Each condom cost $ 0.44 against the $ 0.75 of the product purchased at the vending machine.

My friend immediately bought online and thanked me.

Online you can find many discounts for all products, as well as for compact disc or clothing, just search and be smart.

Use coupons for your purchases. On sites like Groupon, you will find discounts for dinners, restaurants and online shopping. The only thing you will have is the flexibility to use this service when it is available and try to accommodate you, but it is an excellent way to save money without giving up the caprices.

Always consult advertising flyers with supermarket offers. These flyers will become your best allies to save. In this way, you will always know what products are on offer and plan purchases.

Search the Internet for a site or app to control prices across the various physical and online store chains. These sites provide a list of the usual product prices in different stores. In this way, you can decide where to buy the item. A good strategy is to buy all the cheapest items in a store to minimize the impact of shipping costs. It makes no sense to go to a store (using gasoline) to buy a single item; there are no real savings.

The Conclusion

These are just a few tips to adopt a minimalist lifestyle and thus reduce the impact on your monthly budget.

Remember that these tips have a theoretical basis but have to be put into practice in the real world, only do those that have proved useful in your case.

Also, you can always design new ways to save money; you can use these ideas as a good starting point and develop your personal savings system. We will be very curious to know your method if you want to share it.

We have already written that saves can be confused with being stingy.

If you use your brain and our advice, you will never become cheap or comic caricatures, but you can become sources of inspiration for all your friends and family.

Save intelligently and enjoy at the same time of the joys of life is an exciting challenge, but we believe it is a battle that is worth fighting.

We hope our tips are helpful and we are ready to welcome all your feedback.

Thank you all, and good savings!